Engel v. Vitale (1962)

By MARK E. DUDLEY

TWENTY-FIRST CENTURY
BOOKS
A Division of
Henry Holt and Company

New York

To Will, Rik, and Marlene

Twenty-First Century Books
A Division of Henry Holt and Company, Inc.
115 West 18th Street
New York, NY 10011

Henry Holt® and colophon are trademarks of
Henry Holt and Company, Inc.
Publishers since 1866

Published in Canada by Fitzhenry & Whiteside Ltd.
195 Allstate Parkway, Markham, Ontario, L3R 4T8

Library of Congress Cataloging-in-Publication Data
Dudley, Mark E.
Engel v. Vitale (1962) : religion in the schools / Mark E. Dudley. — 1st ed.
p. cm. — (Supreme Court decisions)
Includes bibliographical references and index.
Summary: Points out that although a 1962 Supreme Court case decided that official prayers in public schools are unconstitutional, the issue of separation of church and state remains.
1. Engel, Steven—Trials, litigation, etc.—Juvenile literature. 2. Vitale, William J.—Trials, litigation, etc.—Juvenile literature. 3. Prayer in the public schools—Law and legislation—United States—Juvenile literature. 4. Religion in the public schools—Law and legislation—United States—Juvenile literature. 5. Church and state—United States—Juvenile literature. [1. Engel, Steven—Trials, litigation, etc. 2. Vitale, William J.—Trials, litigation, etc. 3. Religion in the public schools—Law and legislation—United States—Juvenile literature. 4. Church and state.] I. Title. II. Series: Supreme Court decisions (New York, N.Y.)
KF228.E54D83 1995   344.73'0796'0269—dc20   95-19435
[347.3047960269]   CIP AC

Photo Credits
Cartoon on page 12 from *Straight Herblock*, Simon & Schuster, © 1964.
Cartoon on page 15 reprinted with permission, *Chicago Sun Times* © 1995.
Illustrations on pages 18, 22, 27, 30 from North Wind Picture Archives.
Photo on page 39 provided by Bettman Archives.
All other photos provided by AP / Wide World Photos.

Design
Tina Tarr-Emmons

Typesetting and Layout
Custom Communications

ISBN 0-8050-3916-3
First Edition 1995

Printed in the United States of America
All first editions are printed on acid-free paper .

10 9 8 7 6 5 4 3 2 1

Contents

The Bill of Rights

Amendment I

Congress shall make no law respecting an establishment of religion, or prohibiting the free exercise thereof; or abridging the freedom of speech, or of the press; or the right of the people peaceably to assemble, and to petition the Government for a redress of grievances.

Amendment II

A well regulated Militia, being necessary to the security of a free State, the right of the people to keep and bear Arms, shall not be infringed.

Amendment III

No Soldier shall, in time of peace be quartered in any house, without the consent of the Owner, nor in time of war, but in a manner to be prescribed by law.

Amendment IV

The right of the people to be secure in their persons, houses, papers, and effects, against unreasonable searches and seizures, shall not be violated, and no Warrants shall issue, but upon probable cause, supported by Oath or affirmation, and particularly describing the place to be searched, and the persons or things to be seized.

Amendment V

No person shall be held to answer for a capital, or otherwise infamous crime, unless on a presentment or indictment of a Grand Jury, except in cases arising in the land or naval forces, or in the Militia, when in actual service in time of War or public danger; nor shall any person be subject for the same offence to be twice put in jeopardy of life or limb, nor shall be compelled in any criminal case to be a witness against himself, nor be deprived of life, liberty, or property, without due process of law; nor shall private property be taken for public use, without just compensation.

Amendment VI

In all criminal prosecutions, the accused shall enjoy the right to a speedy and public trial, by an impartial jury of the State and district wherein the crime shall have been committed, which district shall have been previously ascertained by law, and to be informed of the nature and cause of the accusation; to be confronted with the witnesses against him; to have compulsory process for obtaining witnesses in his favor, and to have the assistance of counsel for his defence.

Amendment VII

In Suits at common law, where the value in controversy shall exceed twenty dollars, the right of trial by jury shall be preserved, and no fact tried by jury, shall be otherwise reexamined in any Court of the United States, than according to the rules of the common law.

Amendment VIII

Excessive bail shall not be required, nor excessive fines imposed, nor cruel and unusual punishments inflicted.

Amendment IX

The enumeration in the Constitution, of certain rights, shall not be construed to deny or disparage others retained by the people.

Amendment X

The powers not delegated to the United States by the Constitution, nor prohibited by it to the States, are reserved to the States respectively, or to the people.

Amendment XIV (ratified July 28, 1868)

Section 1. All persons born or naturalized in the United States, and subject to the jurisdiction thereof, are citizens of the United States and of the State wherein they reside. No State shall make or enforce any law which shall abridge the privileges or immunities of citizens of the United States; nor shall any State deprive any person of life, liberty, or property, without due process of law; nor deny to any person within its jurisdiction the equal protection of the laws.

Section 2. Representatives shall be apportioned among the several States according to their respective numbers, counting the whole number of persons in each State, excluding Indians not taxed. But when the right to vote at any election for the choice of electors for President and Vice President of the United States, Representatives in Congress, the Executive and Judicial officers of a State, or the members of the Legislature thereof, is denied to any of the male inhabitants of such State, being twenty-one years of age, and citizens of the United States, or in any way abridged, except for participation in rebellion, or other crime, the basis of representation therein shall be reduced in the proportion which the number of such male citizens shall bear to the whole number of male citizens twenty-one years of age in such State.

Section 3. No person shall be a Senator or Representative in Congress, or elector of President and Vice President, or hold any office, civil or military, under the United States, or under any State, who, having previously taken an oath, as a member of Congress, or as an officer of the United States, or as a member of any State legislature, or as an executive or judicial officer of any State, to support the Constitution of the United States, shall have engaged in insurrection or rebellion against the same, or given aid or comfort to the enemies thereof. But Congress may by a vote of two-thirds of each House, remove such disability.

Section 4. The validity of the public debt of the United States, authorized by law, including debts incurred for payments of pensions and bounties for services in suppressing insurrection or rebellion, shall not be questioned. But neither the United States nor any State shall assume or pay any debt or obligation incurred in aid of insurrection or rebellion against the United States, or any claim for the loss or emancipation of any slave; but all such debts, obligations and claims shall be held illegal and void.

Section 5. The Congress shall have power to enforce, by appropriate legislation, the provisions of this article.

Separating Church and State

Almost four centuries ago, the first European settlers came to America seeking refuge from religious persecution. Following the Revolutionary War, the nation's founders sought to guarantee religious freedom for all. The result was the First Amendment to the U.S. Constitution.

This amendment forbids the government from establishing a national religion. It also bars Congress from passing laws that would prevent people from worshiping the way they choose.

The founders knew they could not foresee the nation as it would exist in the years to come. They tried to frame the Constitution in language broad enough to cover unexpected situations. For cases where the Constitution's application was not clear, the founders designated the courts as interpreters of the laws.

Rita Warren of Falls Church, Virginia, carries a mannequin that is supposed to resemble Jesus to her station wagon after a demonstration on the steps of the U.S. Capitol supporting prayer in the schools.

One change that occurred after the signing of the Constitution was the development of the public school system. The few schools that existed in Revolutionary times were operated by towns or churches, not by the federal government. In those schools, moral and religious education went hand in hand with grammar and arithmetic.

As time went on, state and federal governments began to support the schools. By the beginning of the twentieth century, a public school education had become a right of every American child.

The young country, with its vast land, its growing industrial cities, and the promise of liberty, lured immigrants from all over the world to its shores. These immigrants brought their own cultures and religions to America's cities and towns. Public schools that had once been populated almost exclusively by Protestants now had students of diverse faiths.

In many public schools, teachers led students in prayers or Bible readings from the Protestant religion. Parents of other faiths objected to this practice. They did not want their children schooled in a faith other than their own. The parents believed that the government, by funding schools that allowed such practices, was favoring one particular religion over others. That, they claimed, was a violation of the First Amendment.

The Supreme Court heard the parents' complaint in a case known as *Engel v. Vitale*. On June 25, 1962, the Court outlawed officially sanctioned prayer in the schools. The decision focused attention on the First Amendment and its guarantee of freedom of religion. It also drew angry protests from people across the nation.

More than 30 years after the decision, the separation of church and state remains a political issue. Today many politicians, parents, members of the clergy, and other interested parties continue to challenge the ruling as they work to reinstate prayer in public schools.

CHAPTER ONE

The Regents' Prayer

Toleration is not the opposite of intolerance, but it is the counterfeit of it. Both are despotism, the one assumes to itself the right of withholding liberty of conscience, the other of granting it.[1]

—**Thomas Paine**

Joseph and Daniel Roth found their place in history a most uncomfortable one. Walking home from their school in New Hyde Park on Long Island, New York, in 1959, the young brothers were often taunted by their schoolmates.

"Hey, you Jew bastard!"[2] they would call. The Irish and Italian boys would jokingly cross themselves in the manner of their Catholic faith when they passed the Roth brothers. Joe and Daniel defended themselves as best they could. Sometimes they got into fistfights. At home, they sulked, angry that their parents' beliefs caused them to be treated as outcasts.

What Lawrence Roth, their father, believed was that public schools had no business promoting religion. "It all began," Lawrence Roth said,

This cartoon was published in the *Washington Post* after people protested the U.S. Supreme Court ruling banning prayer in public schools.

"with a teacher who kept a statue of Christ in her third grade room. If you were bad, she would say, you would be punished by Christ."[3]

The Roths were Jewish, but they didn't practice any religious faith. Nevertheless, Lawrence was offended that the Christian God was included in his children's education. Many other parents in the neighborhood felt the same way, regardless of their faith.

Roth decided to get more involved after a decision by the local school board. School District No. 9, known as the Herricks school system, governed the towns of New Hyde Park, Manhasset, Albertson, Roslyn, Roslyn Heights, and Williston. The board instructed the teachers in the district to lead their classes in prayer every morning.

The New York State Board of Regents had recommended a prayer for use in all public schools in 1951. Mary Harte, a Regents board member, had tried for three years to introduce the prayer into the schools' curriculum. Finally, in 1958, she succeeded. The prayer read, "Almighty God, we acknowledge our dependence upon Thee, and we beg Thy blessings upon us, our parents, our teachers and our Country."[4]

Participation in the prayer was not mandatory. However, students not taking part were expected to leave the room. The policy forced the children to reveal their religious beliefs. The vast majority of the students in the district belonged to Christian sects that favored the prayer. Even if reciting the prayer was against their beliefs, children tended to bend to peer pressure and remain in the classroom.

The coercive nature of the exercise disturbed the elder Roth. He asked his boys to leave the room during the prayer. When they did, they were singled out as troublemakers and ridiculed as outsiders. Even some teachers harassed the Roth boys.

Roth asked the American Civil Liberties Union (ACLU) for help. The

Burck in The Chicago Sun-Times

"The 11th commandment."

This cartoon appeared on the editorial page of the *New York Times* the Sunday after the *Engel v. Vitale* decision was announced by the Supreme Court.

nonprofit association assisted various causes in support of the individual liberties guaranteed by the U.S. Constitution. The most important of these rights are the first ten amendments, called the Bill of Rights. The first of these reads, "Congress shall make no law respecting an establishment of religion, or prohibiting the free exercise thereof."[5]

Roth believed that by introducing the Regents' prayer, the Herricks school board was violating the first part of the amendment. The nation's founders had passed the amendment to ensure that the federal government would not establish an official national religion. They believed such matters were best left to one's own conscience. They thought it would be too easy for members of a state church, with the power of the federal government behind them, to suppress other religions or discriminate against their members.

Although the Regents' prayer was not from any particular religious sect, Roth thought it was not appropriate for everyone in the district. Praying together implied that all the students prayed to the same deity. Even the word *God* suggested devotion to the Christian or Jewish faith. Members of the Muslim faith, for example, call their deity Allah.

Some other religions don't recognize the concept of a Supreme Being. Atheists and other nonbelievers deserved to have their rights protected, too. Even some Christian sects objected to the wording of the prayer. Many Lutherans, for example, believe that all prayers must be made "in the name of Jesus."[6]

The ACLU agreed with Roth. They encouraged him to organize other parents in the district who believed as he did. Roth placed an ad in the local paper:

> Notice: To all Herrick's [sic] school district
> taxpayers: A taxpayers suit will soon be
> started to challenge the legality of prayers
> in public schools. Counsel has been appointed.
>
> All interested parties CALL:
> Lawrence Roth
> 555-7652 AFTER 5 P.M. DAILY[7]

About 50 citizens answered the ad. They didn't want the school board telling their children how and when to pray. As the ACLU prepared the lawsuit, the number of people participating in the suit dwindled. Some dropped out in the face of criticism from their neighbors or the clergy. Others weren't included because their children would be too old by the time the case was heard. Most lawsuits take years to resolve. It would be best if the plaintiffs' children were still in school at the time of the case's conclusion.

Several months after Roth placed the ad, five parents were selected as the plaintiffs. A plaintiff is the person or group bringing a complaint before a court. They were Roth, David Lichtenstein, Monroe Lerner, Leonore Lyons, and Steven Engel. The plaintiffs were listed alphabetically, so it was Engel's name that would identify the suit.

Soon the group presented their demands to the president of the Herricks school board. William Vitale was served a petition asking for a hearing before the New York Supreme Court. This case, *Engel v. Vitale*, would eventually make its way through the court system to the U.S. Supreme Court and one day change the law of the land.

CHAPTER TWO

In the Beginning

We hold these truths to be self-evident, that all men are created equal, that they are endowed by their Creator with certain unalienable Rights, that among these are Life, Liberty and the pursuit of Happiness.[1]

—The Declaration of Independence

The first European settlers of the land that would become the United States owed their religious heritage to the Judeo-Christian tradition. Of particular importance to U.S. history was the rise of Calvinism in Switzerland in the 1540s. John Calvin taught that God's wrath would be brought upon any community that tolerated nonbelievers and sinners. Therefore, it was the responsibility of the government to suppress religious dissent. "The punishments executed upon false prophets, and seducing teachers, do bring down the showers of God's blessings upon the civil state,"[2] Calvin wrote.

Calvinism became the basis for the beliefs of the Puritans and the

John Calvin, sixteenth-century theologian and religious reformer

Pilgrims, two of the most prominent groups first to settle New England. The Pilgrims were a group of Protestants from Nottingham, England, who wished to separate from the Church of England. At first they moved to Amsterdam and later to Leiden in the Netherlands. That country allowed freedom of religion, and the Pilgrims prospered. Unhappy that their children were learning Dutch ways, they moved back to England after ten years. There they sought permission to settle the New World. Landing in Plymouth, in what is now Massachusetts, in 1620, they founded a colony. True to their Calvinist origins, they sought not to establish a society where religious tolerance was encouraged, but a community where only their beliefs were practiced.

The Puritans, another group of Protestants, settled Boston ten years later and were even more intolerant of other sects. They believed that the Church of England was corrupt. By moving to America, they hoped to purify Church practices. The Puritans forced everyone in the colony to attend church. Only members of the church were allowed to vote or hold public office. They required strict adherence to Church law. Especially vilified were the Protestant sects whose beliefs strayed further from mainstream doctrines, such as Unitarians and Quakers. The few Quakers who ventured to Massachusetts Bay Colony were often branded, had their ears cut off, were sold as servants, or even killed outright.

Still, there was some dissent. Roger Williams, a young minister, criticized the Puritans for not breaking completely with the Church of England. He also protested the Puritans' oppression of the local Native Americans and members of other religious sects. Williams believed in the separation of church and state. He thought that human experience was divided into the world of nature, including political and civil life, and the world of spirit. Williams preached that those two worlds couldn't mix.

One's religion was a matter between a person and God. He believed men and women should be free to worship as they pleased.

In 1634, Native American tribes siding with the Canadian French, who were expanding into the settlers' territory, began threatening English settlements. In response, the Puritans required all Massachusetts citizens to swear an oath of loyalty, in the name of God. Williams thought this was an unacceptable use of God's name for civil concerns. He refused to take the oath.

The Puritans banished Williams from their colony. After briefly living with a Native American tribe, he bought land in what was to become Providence, Rhode Island, and established a colony. Williams allowed members of all faiths to settle there. He let a group of Quakers move there, though he thought their beliefs were sinful. Even non-Christians were welcome. The first synagogue in America was established in Newport, Rhode Island, in 1763.

As religious refugees fled to the area, nearby settlements banded together to form the Providence Plantations. In 1663, Rhode Island was granted a royal charter. It stated that "no person within the said Colony, at any time hereafter, shall be in any wise molested, punished, disquieted or called in question for any differences in opinions in matters of religion," and that all would "at all times hereafter, freely and fully have and enjoy . . . their own judgments and consciences, in matters of religious concernments."[3]

Meanwhile, the colonization of America continued. Most of the early settlements were founded by people seeking to worship as they pleased. Lord Baltimore, a Roman Catholic, settled in Maryland, providing one of the few areas where Catholics were welcome. He allowed members of other Christian faiths (except Unitarians) to settle there as well. Twenty years

Governor Peter Stuyvesant surrendering New Netherland to the English

later, the Unitarians, who did not believe in the Trinity, were allowed to settle there, too.

As their population grew, Puritans began to move to Maryland in greater numbers. Eventually, the Puritans gained control and outlawed both the Roman Catholic Church and the Church of England. But Kings Charles II and James II reasserted British authority over the colonies, and the Church of England became Maryland's official church.

In New York, formerly called New Netherland, Governor Peter Stuyvesant established the Dutch Reformed Church as the state religion. Baptists, Lutherans, Quakers, Catholics, and Jews were "actively persecuted."[4] After the Duke of York took over the colony from the Dutch, things became slightly better. The Duke gave each town the power to choose a minister for its church—as long as he was of the Protestant faith. Protestant churches were supported by taxes collected by the civil authorities.

Catholics and Jews were allowed to live and worship in New York. To become citizens, however, Catholics were required to renounce their allegiance to the Pope. Jews were given the rights of citizens for a time during the last half of the 1600s, but their citizenship rights were later revoked when the political mood changed.

From the late 1600s onward, religious tolerance grew. Massachusetts granted religious freedom to "all Christians (except Papists [Roman Catholics])"[5] in 1691. Connecticut and New Hampshire followed suit.

Improved roads, better mail service, and increasing trade linked formerly isolated communities. Newspapers and pamphlets espousing different ideas began circulating. Colleges were founded. Towns established elementary schools for their children. As towns spread across the land, more people lived in the country, out of easy reach of the churches. By 1800, only about 10 percent of U.S. citizens belonged to a church. Historians have found that "the great majority of Americans in the eighteenth century were outside any church, and there was an overwhelming indifference to religion."[6]

Despite this, the religious convictions of the people were not something the American leaders could ignore. Following the expulsion of the British in the American Revolution, the new states were hardly unified. As they struggled to form a nation, local legislatures wanted to ensure that the religious rights of their constituents would not be trampled. Having recently won their independence from the British, the states wanted assurances that the more populous or powerful states would not restrict their freedom. To guarantee that, delegates from the 13 former colonies met to formulate a written constitution, listing their rights and responsibilities. That was a novel idea—in fact, the United States has the world's oldest written constitution.

The 55 delegates who met at the Constitutional Convention in Philadelphia in May 1787 were of many faiths. They represented a population of four million, consisting of dozens of Protestant sects, as well as approximately 25,000 Catholics and 10,000 Jews. It was no surprise that a great majority opposed the establishment of a national church. Some leaders who owed their power to their church may have wished to see such an institution. However, they were afraid that the national religion selected would not be their own. The Congregationalists of New England as well as the Anglicans of the South were not inclined to give up the power that went with their dominance.

Many of the delegates believed that religious convictions should remain a private concern. However, Benjamin Franklin, the most respected elder statesman at the convention, suggested that "henceforth prayer imploring the assistance of Heaven, and its blessing on our deliberations, be held in this Assembly every morning before we proceed to business."[7] The delegates sat in embarrassed silence. They considered Franklin's ideas on prayer quaintly outdated.

Compromise was essential if the colonies were to band together against their common enemies. The Constitutional Congress did not go smoothly. Many delegates refused to sign the completed document or even to attend. In order to make the text of the Constitution more palatable to everyone, almost all mention of religion was left out. The oath of office of the president, "I do solemnly swear (or affirm) that I will faithfully execute the office of President of the United States . . ."[8] was worded that way to eliminate the objections of those who, like Roger Williams, refused to swear an oath for a civil matter.

Article VI, paragraph 3 of the Constitution also provides for either oath or affirmation. It goes on to state, "no religious Test shall ever be required as a Qualification to any Office or public Trust under the United States."[9] Charles Pinckney, a delegate from South Carolina, introduced the measure to stop discrimination against members of minority faiths. Despite the fact that several states had just such a requirement for public office, there was little debate about banning the federal government from requiring a religious test.

When Pinckney suggested a clause forbidding congressional interference in religious disputes, he found no support, though. James Madison, the principal author of the Constitution, thought such a directive was so obvious that no clause was needed. Alexander Hamilton, a delegate from New York, thought the Constitution shouldn't specify any actions the federal government could or could not take regarding religion. That, he argued, would create the impression it was all right for Congress to legislate other religious matters not mentioned in the Constitution. Other delegates agreed.

Many delegates, however, wanted citizens' rights to freedom of religion spelled out, not just implied. George Mason, a delegate from Virginia, wouldn't sign the Constitution without assurances of religious liberty and the separation of affairs between church and state.

Finally the delegates approved the Constitution and sent it to the states for ratification. Acceptance was by no means universal. Delegates from neither Rhode Island nor North Carolina would sign. Six other states signed, but they submitted proposals for a Bill of Rights to accompany the document. Eventually, nine states ratified the Constitution, and it went into effect on March 4, 1789. Work began immediately on a Bill of Rights.

Of highest concern to the founders was the question of religious liberty. Accordingly, Madison addressed that issue first as he prepared a draft of the Bill of Rights. The roots of the First Amendment can be found in the early proceedings of the Virginia State Legislature. In 1776, that state passed a Declaration of Rights, guaranteeing freedom of religion to its citizens. It stated, "That religion, or the duty which we owe to our Creator, and the manner of discharging it, can be directed only by reason and conviction, not by force or violence; and, therefore, all men are equally entitled to the free exercise of religion, according to the dictates of conscience."[10]

Several years later, however, Patrick Henry proposed a bill assessing a tax on the populace "for the support of the Christian religion, or of some Christian church."[11] Madison and Thomas Jefferson protested the bill. Madison outlined his opposition in his "Memorial and Remonstrance Against Religious Assessments":

> We remonstrate against said Bill . . . Because
> we hold it for a fundamental and undeniable
> truth, "that religion, or the duty which we owe
> to our Creator, and the manner of discharging
> it, can be directed only by reason and convic-
> tion, not by force or violence." The religion
> then of every man must be left to the conviction
> and conscience of every man; and it is the right
> of every man to exercise it as these may dictate.
> This right is in its nature an unalienable right.
> It is unalienable; because the opinions of men,
> depending only on the evidence contemplated
> by their own minds, cannot follow the dictates
> of other men; it is unalienable also; because
> what is here a right towards men, is a duty

James Madison, 1751-1836, statesman and fourth president of the United States

towards the Creator. It is the duty of every
man to render to the Creator such homage, and
such only, as he believes to be acceptable to
him. This duty is precedent both in order of
time and degree of obligation to the claims of
Civil Society.[12]

Madison went on:

The same authority which can establish Christianity, in exclusion of all other religions, may

establish with the same ease any particular sect
of Christians in exclusion of all other sects, and
the same authority which can force a citizen to
contribute three pence only of his property for
the support of any one establishment, may
force him to conform to any other establishment in all cases whatsoever.[13]

The argument went on for several years. In 1786 the bill was defeated,
and Virginia adopted Jefferson's Bill for Establishing Religious Freedom.
The preamble states, "It is sinful and tyrannical to compel a man to furnish
contributions for the propagation of opinions which he disbelieves and
abhors; and it is also wrong to force him to support this or that teacher of
his own religious persuasion."[14]

The bill goes on directing that:

No one would be forced to attend or support
any religious worship or ministry and that no
one would be restrained, molested, fined or
made to suffer in any manner because of his
religious opinions or beliefs. Everyone would
be free to argue and to maintain their own
opinions in matters of religion with no effect
upon their civil capacity.[15]

Madison drew upon these arguments when he wrote the First Amendment. His first draft read, "The civil rights of none shall be abridged on

account of religious belief, nor shall any national religion be established, nor shall the full and equal rights of conscience in any manner or on any pretext be infringed."[16]

The members of the First Congress criticized this form for the same reasons Hamilton had argued against Pinckney's proposed clause. Such a specific listing of the federal government's powers regarding religion left the door open for later abuses. After some discussion, the amendment was presented in the broader, and vaguer, prohibition, "Congress shall make no law respecting an establishment of religion, or prohibiting the free exercise thereof."[17]

This was really two prohibitions. The first part of the sentence became known as the "establishment clause." Its intent was to prevent the federal government from favoring any one church by officially supporting it. The second part was known as the "free exercise clause." It barred federal authorities from interfering in people's practice of their religion.

This was the form accepted when Congress passed the Bill of Rights on September 25, 1789. The states ratified the ten amendments before Christmas of that year. Religious freedom was now a guaranteed right to all citizens.

CHAPTER THREE

From First to Fourteenth

There is no country in the world in which the Christian religion retains a greater influence over the souls of men than in America.[1]

—**Alexis de Tocqueville**

Approval of the First Amendment did not mean that there would be no government involvement with citizens' religious activities. When George Washington took office in 1789, one of his first acts, at the request of Congress, was to declare a day of national thanksgiving and prayer. Washington was a member of Christ Church in Alexandria, Virginia, but rarely attended services. Like Jefferson and Madison, he considered himself a Deist. Deists believe their relationship with the Creator is a personal one, not a matter for organized religion.

However, Washington recognized that although few people of the time belonged to churches, nearly everyone believed in God. Six months after

George Washington taking the oath as president of the United States on April 30, 1789

taking office, President Washington issued the National Thanksgiving Proclamation:

> Whereas it is the duty of all nations to acknowledge the providence of Almighty God, to obey His will, to be grateful for His benefits, and humbly to implore His protection and favor . . . Now, therefore, I do recommend and assign Thursday, the 26th day of November next, to be devoted by people of these States to the service of that great and glorious Being . . . And also that we may then unite in most humbly offering our prayers and supplications to the great Lord and Ruler of nations, and beseech Him to pardon our national and other transgressions.[2]

Washington also approved the use of public funds to pay the clerics who began each session of Congress with a prayer and for Armed Services chaplains. He still resisted any official link of the U.S. government to a specific religion, though. In an official proclamation in 1796, Washington stated, "The Government of the United States of America is not in any sense founded on the Christian religion."[3]

Two U.S. presidents—Jefferson and Madison—believed the restrictions of the First Amendment prevented them from proclaiming religious holidays. Jefferson stated his beliefs on the proper relationship between church and state with a now famous analogy. Writing to the Connecticut Baptists Association of Danbury in 1802, President Jefferson said:

Believing with you that religion is a matter which lies solely between man and his God, that he owes account to none other for his faith or his worship, that the legislative powers of government reach actions only, and not opinions, I contemplate with sovereign reverence that act of the whole American people which declared that their legislature should "make no law respecting an establishment of religion, or prohibiting the free exercise thereof," thus building a wall of separation between Church and State.[4]

Jefferson drew his analogy from the words of Roger Williams. Almost two centuries earlier, Williams had written of the "hedge or wall of separation between the garden of the church and the wilderness of the world."[5] Ever since, the "wall of separation" has been the key phrase describing the relationship between government and religion.

Though the First Amendment protected citizens from federal interference in their religious beliefs, states were still free to regulate churches. Massachusetts, Connecticut, New Hampshire, and Maryland had official state churches after the Constitution was ratified. In 1833 Massachusetts finally broke its connection with the Congregationalists. Until then, towns were required to hire Protestant teachers to teach religion. Even after Connecticut officially broke off from the Congregationalist church in 1818, state taxes supported the church until 1868.

Non-Protestants didn't hold full civil rights in New Jersey until 1844. Neither Jews nor Catholics could vote in New Hampshire until 1851. They weren't allowed to hold office in that state until 1876. In the same year, Maryland finally granted full civil rights to Jews and Unitarians.

Often, these laws were ignored. In North Carolina, a Jew was elected to the state legislature in 1808. Officially, Jews weren't allowed to run for office there until 1868. Discriminatory laws remained on the books, though. They became convenient tools to be used against immigrants who practiced other religions.

As economic upheaval and religious persecution uprooted millions in Europe, immigrants poured into the United States. The largest groups consisted of Catholics from Ireland and Germany and Jews routed from Russia and Eastern Europe. Arriving in America almost penniless, these groups usually settled in the cities of the East.

Competition for jobs between the immigrants and native-born Americans sometimes erupted into violent clashes. These disputes in turn led to increased prejudice and discrimination. The predominant Protestants worried that the Catholics would become a dominant force in local politics. Many feared the Catholics would honor their allegiance to the Pope over bonds to their new homeland.

Another area of conflict developed in the schools. Until the mid-1800s, few schools were operated by the states. Usually, churches conducted children's education. As the nation's economy turned from a rural, agricultural base to an urban, industrial one, more children were sent to school. When states took over the task of education, they built on the structure begun by the churches. Secular and religious education blended.

As a result, the new immigrants' children were often instructed in Protestant beliefs. Catholics and other religious groups protested, but they lacked the votes to change these practices. To prevent their children from being brought up Protestant, Catholics began their own schools. These parochial schools rarely could compete with the quality of public schools, though, since they lacked the tax dollars to support them.

Soon the parochial schools turned to the courts in an attempt to receive public funding for textbooks and supplies. Many regarded this as an attack on Protestantism. Anti-Catholic fervor grew. Mobs burned parochial schools and drove priests from towns. Catholic children were expelled from public schools for refusing to take part in Protestant religious exercises.

Non-Christians fared little better. Although their smaller numbers made them less feared than Catholics, they were met with ignorance and misunderstanding. Authorities justified discriminatory policies by saying that the United States was a "Christian nation." In 1843, when Jews in New York City asked that their children not be taught lessons from the New Testament, the Board of Education saw no problem with the schools' teachings. After all, they told the parents, the schools were only trying to "inculcate general principles of Christianity."[6]

Federal authorities could do little to help. In an 1845 ruling, the U.S. Supreme Court made it clear that the federal government couldn't interfere with the states' authority. In *Permoli v. First Municipality No. 1 of New Orleans*, the plaintiffs asked the Court to rule a city law forbidding open-casket funerals as unconstitutional. The plaintiffs believed such a law violated their free exercise of religion.

The Court ruled, "The Constitution of 1789 makes no provision for protecting the citizens of the respective states in their religious liberties; this is left to the state constitutions and laws."[7]

On the national scene, the mood was hardly right for protecting the rights of religious minorities. Major political parties and civic clubs were organized for the purpose of keeping Catholics from power. Protestant leaders founded the National Reform Association, proposing to add an amendment to the Constitution establishing the United States as a "Christian nation." They suggested the Preamble to the Constitution be changed to read:

> Recognizing Almighty God as the source of all
> authority and power in civil government, and
> acknowledging the Lord Jesus Christ as the
> governor among the nations, His revealed will
> as the supreme law of our land, in order to
> Constitute a Christian government.[8]

The effect of the Bill of Rights on the states changed in the aftermath of the Civil War. To protect Southern blacks from discrimination after they were granted citizenship, Congress passed the Fourteenth Amendment in 1868. The amendment states, "No State shall make or enforce any law which shall abridge the privileges or immunities of citizens of the United States."[9]

Some politicians and legal experts have interpreted the Fourteenth Amendment as guaranteeing the rights outlined in the Bill of Rights to the citizens of every state. They argue that, under the terms of the Fourteenth Amendment, the Bill of Rights applies to the states as well as to the federal government.

The issue has come before the Supreme Court many times. The Court has never stated that the Fourteenth Amendment requires the states to abide by the entire Bill of Rights. Nevertheless, in individual cases, the Court has ruled that some of those rights—including those guaranteed in the First Amendment—are due every U.S. citizen.

CHAPTER FOUR

God and the Flag

*Render therefore to Caesar the things
that are Caesar's, and to God the
things that are God's.[1]*

—Matthew 22:21

The nation's founders entrusted the Supreme Court
with guarding citizens' rights, but the Court's rulings sometimes are seen
as violating that trust. Critics charged that an 1878 ruling by the Supreme
Court weakened the First Amendment's guarantee of religious freedom.

In *Reynolds v. United States*, the Court upheld a federal law that
banned the Mormon practice of polygamy, or having more than one spouse.
The Court said that free exercise of religion applied only to beliefs and not
to religious practices, such as multiple marriages. "Laws are made for the
government of actions," said Chief Justice Morrison R. Waite, "and while
they cannot interfere with mere religious belief and opinions, they may with
practices."[2]

The First Amendment's wording, however, guarantees "free exercise." Critics of the ruling protested that "free exercise" meant practices as
well as beliefs.

In the 1890 decision *Davis v. Beason*, the Court went a step further in stripping the free exercise clause of its meaning. The justices upheld the conviction of a man charged under a law denying the vote to those who supported polygamy, even if they didn't practice it themselves. There was no proof that the defendant promoted polygamy. It was enough that he belonged to the Mormon religion, which advocated polygamy—even though it had been declared illegal some 12 years before.

By 1940, the Supreme Court justices had shied away from the labored reasoning behind the *Reynolds* and *Davis* decisions. They continued to rule against unusual beliefs, however. The Gobitas children could testify to that.

William and Lillian Gobitas had been expelled from the Minersville Public School System in the hills of east-central Pennsylvania in 1935. The children had refused to participate in the daily school exercise of reciting the Pledge of Allegiance and saluting the American flag. Their parents said such a requirement violated their beliefs as Jehovah's Witnesses.

Jehovah's Witnesses believe that the Lord's instructions in the Bible forbid them from saluting a flag—a graven image in their eyes. Ten-year-old William described his belief in a letter to school authorities:

> Dear Sirs, I do not salute the flag because
> I have promised to do the will of God. That
> means that I must not worship anything out of
> harmony with God's law. In the twentieth
> chapter of Exodus it is stated, "Thou shalt
> not make unto thee any graven image nor bow
> down to them nor serve them. . . ." I do not
> salute the flag [not] because I do not love

Walter Gobitas, center, leaves the U.S. District Court in Philadelphia with his children, William and Lillian, after a hearing on the students' refusal to salute the flag.

my country but [because] I love my country
and I love God more and I must abide by His
commandments.

—Your pupil, Billy Gobitas[3]

His parents explained further: "We are not desecrating the American
flag or even speaking against it. We show no disrespect in any way for the
flag, but we cannot salute it. We simply cannot take an oath to anything or

any person—only to Jehovah [the Old Testament's name for God]. The Bible tells us this, and we must obey."[4]

The Gobitases' situation was not unique. Jehovah's Witnesses throughout the country suffered harassment at the hands of local authorities and townspeople. State courts consistently ruled against the Witnesses. The courts viewed such cases as having more to do with patriotism than with religion. In a New Jersey case, the judge wrote, "The pledge of allegiance is, by no stretch of the imagination, a religious rite. . . . Those who do not desire to conform with the demands of the statute [law on flag saluting] can seek their schooling elsewhere."[5]

Many Witnesses had done just that, by forming their own schools that required no saluting. For many others, though, this was impossible.

Olin R. Moyle, the Witnesses' attorney, presented the Gobitas case to Judge Albert Maris of the U.S. District Court for the Eastern District of Pennsylvania. Moyle's written argument, called a brief, claimed the Minersville School Board had violated the Gobitases' rights under the Fourteenth Amendment. He said the board had no right to force the children to violate their religious beliefs since the flag salute "does not and cannot affect the public interest or safety of others."[6]

In a pretrial ruling, Judge Maris was sympathetic to the Gobitases' cause. He wrote, "Individuals have the right not only to entertain any religious belief but also to do or refrain from doing any act on conscientious grounds, which does not prejudice the safety, morals, property or personal rights of the people."[7]

The Gobitases' case began receiving more publicity after Philadelphia newspapers printed Judge Maris's words. The state's superintendent of schools commented that forcing students to salute the flag was something more suitable for the dictatorships in Germany and Italy than for the

United States. On the other hand, patriotic organizations like the American Legion supported a mandatory salute and offered financial help for the school district's legal battle.

During the trial, the plaintiffs said they believed that by saluting the flag, they would violate the Bible's Second Commandment. The commandment tells followers not to make "graven images" and not to "bow down" or serve such images. The flag, the plaintiffs argued, was a graven image. To salute it in defiance of the Second Commandment, they said, would result in eternal damnation.

In turn, Superintendent Charles Roudabush, representing the Minersville School District, related his fears. He said the Gobitas children's refusal to salute the flag would affect other schoolchildren. "The tendency would be to spread," Roudabush told the court. "In our mixed population where we have foreigners of every variety, it would be no time until they would form a dislike, a disregard for our flag and country."[8]

Judge Maris eventually ruled in favor of the Gobitas children. On June 18, 1938, he ordered the school district to take the children back at the start of the next school year. They would not be required to salute the flag. Roudabush was bitter over the decision. "Boys and girls who do not acknowledge allegiance to their country of birth are aliens, and do not belong in the public schools which are tax supported,"[9] he told the local paper.

Roudabush convinced the school board to appeal Judge Maris's ruling to the Court of Appeals for the Third Circuit. There, the board's lawyers tried to convince the three-judge panel that Judge Maris had erred in ruling that the flag salute could have a religious significance. The attorneys also argued that the public good was better served by requiring acts of patriotism such as flag salutes.

The circuit court ruled for the Gobitases. The written opinion commented that Adolf Hitler also persecuted the Jehovah's Witnesses and confiscated their property and literature. The judges noted the insincerity of forced patriotism. They cited the history of religious persecution in the founding of the colonies and in Pennsylvania in particular. The opinion concluded by quoting George Washington: "I assure you very explicitly, that in my opinion the conscientious scruples of all men should be treated with great delicacy and tenderness."[10] The judges found this delicacy lacking in the school board's actions.

The school board wasn't ready to give up. There was one course of action left. The board voted to appeal the circuit court's decision to the U.S. Supreme Court.

The Supreme Court was by no means duty bound to accept the Gobitas case for argument. The Court accepts only a fraction of appeals each year. In fact, three cases involving refusals to salute by Jehovah's Witnesses had been turned down by the Court in recent years.

(*Gobitas* is the correct spelling of the name. Unfortunately, it was spelled *Gobitis* in the initial legal documents. The misspelling remained in the Supreme Court case title and most subsequent sources.)

By 1940, the year the *Minersville School District v. Gobitis* case reached the Supreme Court, the time was right for the justices to address the issue. Hundreds of Jehovah's Witnesses children had been expelled from schools in the 18 states requiring flag salutes. Rulings by the lower federal courts favoring the Witnesses also influenced the justices' decision to take the case.

Unfortunately for the Gobitases, Moyle was replaced with Joseph Rutherford as their lawyer. Rutherford, the leader of America's Jehovah's Witnesses at the time, decided he should take charge of the high-profile case. Though an attorney, Rutherford alienated the justices by lecturing them. His brief seemed more an attempt to preach his religion than to convince the Court by intellectual reasoning that his clients' constitutional rights were being violated.

Two amicus curiae briefs, from the ACLU and the American Bar Association, were more helpful to the Gobitases' case. *Amicus curiae* means "friend of the court." The term refers to interested parties who argue on one side or the other of a case before the Court. The Supreme Court, when reviewing a case, may use arguments in the amicus curiae briefs in reaching its decision. The ACLU and ABA briefs emphasized America's heritage of religious freedom.

Cases are presented to the Supreme Court in two stages. First the various parties present their written arguments, the briefs. These cite any related rulings set by past Court decisions, known as precedents. Briefs also give reasons why those opinions should apply to the current case.

Next the Court holds a hearing for oral arguments. Each side is given a limited time to defend its position. The lawyers answer questions the justices ask them. The attorneys also rebut each other's arguments.

Rutherford argued in behalf of the Gobitases for one-half hour. George Gardner, who presented the arguments of the ACLU brief, spoke for an additional half hour. This was an unusual step. Usually, amicus curiae submit only written briefs. In this case, though, the Court decided that the ACLU's testimony would be useful.

Rutherford's time at the podium didn't go well. The justices have little patience for speeches. They want to hear logical arguments based on legal precedents. Rutherford spent his half hour preaching as though he were in his church. The justices responded with silence.

Gardner tried his best to make up for Rutherford. He addressed only the constitutional issues. The justices badgered him with questions. Associate Justice Felix Frankfurter, in particular, relentlessly challenged Gardner's reasoning.

The school board's lawyers concentrated on presenting their arguments as briefly as possible. They stuck to their contention that Minersville had done nothing to violate the Constitution. The justices accepted their presentation with few interruptions or questions.

Despite the poor showing made by the Gobitases' advocates, they believed that the Court would rule in their favor. Usually, the justices are influenced more by the briefs than by oral arguments. During the two months between the hearing and the announcement of the Court's decision, the Gobitases were encouraged by another court case.

In *Cantwell v. Connecticut*, the Court overturned a Jehovah's Witness's conviction for breach of peace. Jesse Cantwell was arrested after broadcasting anti-Catholic messages in a heavily Catholic New Haven, Connecticut, neighborhood. Cantwell appealed, claiming his First and Fourteenth Amendment rights had been violated. The Court's decision was the first to apply the free exercise clause to the states.

Despite the positive signs, the Court ruled against the Gobitases. The justices decided that the law requiring schoolchildren to salute the flag had not been made with any restrictions on religious beliefs in mind. Therefore, they stated, the law was not unconstitutional. Just because the law conflicted with a religious sect's practices was no reason to excuse members of that sect from obeying it, the Court ruled.

The justices believed that patriotism was more important than religious freedom. Patriotism was much on the minds of the nation's leaders in 1940. Many people considered the disruptive labor movement in the United States to be influenced by Communists backed by the Soviet Union. The growing threat of Hitler's Germany also encouraged nationalistic sentiments. Many people viewed a refusal to salute the flag as a threat to national security.

Throughout its annual term, which usually runs from October to late June or early July, the Court votes on the cases it has heard. The vote need not be unanimous—a simple majority carries the full authority of the Court. Generally, if the chief justice votes with the majority, he writes the opinion himself or assigns the task to an associate justice. If the chief justice does not vote with the majority, the associate who has been on the Court the longest, and who votes with the majority, assigns the opinion.

The decision is read aloud in court for the benefit of the public and the reporters present. The written text of the opinion is distributed at the same time. Justices who disagree with the decision are free to present their reasons at this time. This is known as a dissent. Justices who agree with the opinion, but want to explain their vote, may issue a concurrence.

Chief Justice Charles Evans Hughes assigned the *Gobitis* opinion to Justice Frankfurter. The opinion emphasized the need to bow to the greater good in promoting patriotism over religious freedom. Frankfurter recognized that balancing the common good with individual liberties was a delicate task. He referred to the problem by quoting Abraham Lincoln's words: "Must a government of necessity be too strong for the liberties of its people, or too weak to maintain its own existence?"[11]

At the end of the opinion, Frankfurter said the Court believed that such issues of religious freedom should be decided by the states, not the courts. If the people were dissatisfied with the law, they could change the law, he said. Frankfurter wrote that he wanted "to use this opinion as a vehicle for preaching the true democratic faith of not relying on the Court for the impossible task of assuring a vigorous, mature, self-protecting and tolerant democracy by bringing responsibility . . . directly home where it belongs—to the people and their representatives themselves."[12]

There was one dissenting vote. Justice Harlan F. Stone read his dissent after Frankfurter announced the Court's opinion. He believed the Minersville flag salute law hindered freedom of speech and freedom of religion. He thought the law violated the First and Fourteenth Amendments. Stone said the other justices recognized these violations and overlooked them, claiming that their action served the country better. He reminded them that, historically, governments that suppressed individual liberties usually justified their actions by claiming to support the public good.

Stone believed the founders' major concern was the rights of individuals. He said the constitutional provisions protected these liberties:

> The very essence of the liberty which they
> guarantee is the freedom of the individual
> from compulsion as to what he shall think
> and what he shall say, at least where the
> compulsion is to bear false witness to his
> religion. If these guarantees are to have
> any meaning they must, I think . . . withhold
> from the state any authority to compel belief
> or the expression of it where that expression
> violates religious convictions, whatever may
> be the legislative view of the desirability
> of such compulsion.[13]

Finally, Stone chided his fellow justices for believing that democracy

Police escort Jehovah's Witnesses into a police car to protect them from an unfriendly crowd during the 1940s.

would be strengthened by the *Gobitis* decision. Allowing the legislature to decide if national security justified suppressing the Jehovah's Witnesses religious convictions was unfair, he said. There were too few Witnesses to sway the opinion of the majority. It was precisely the role of the courts, he said, to prevent mob rule from trampling the rights of powerless minorities.

The *Gobitis* decision galvanized the Witnesses' enemies. They spread rumors that the Witnesses were really spies intent on subversion and sabotage. Within two weeks of the announcement of the Court's decision, mobs throughout the United States attacked the Witnesses. They were shot at, beaten, and tarred and feathered. Their homes, cars, and meeting halls were burned. Police frequently joined the mobs or arrested the victims.

The Supreme Court decision was criticized by the newspapers and many political leaders. As stories of the Witnesses' persecution spread, the nation's courts, if not its people, began to favor the Witnesses. Usually, lower courts are guided by Supreme Court opinions. This time, however, court after court ignored the *Gobitis* ruling and directed that Witnesses' children be allowed to attend school unmolested without saluting the flag.

By June 1942, the Supreme Court seemed ready to admit its error in a related suit. The case, *Jones v. City of Opelika*, involved local laws requiring Witnesses to obtain permits to distribute their literature. Although the opinion of the Court went against the Witnesses, the vote was close—five to four. Three of the justices who had voted against the Gobitases' cause now signed a dissent that read, "This is but another step in the direction which *Minersville School District v. Gobitis* took against the same religious minority and is a logical extension of the principles upon which that decision rested. Since we joined in the opinion in the *Gobitis* case, we think this an appropriate occasion to state that we now believe that it was also wrongly decided."[14]

It was almost unheard-of for justices to admit a mistake. The Supreme Court is always reluctant to overturn precedents. The principle of following precedent is called stare decisis. The term derives from a Latin phrase *stare decisis, et non quieta movere*. This means "to stand by decisions and not disturb settled matters."[15]

Laws that remain constant allow society to function in an orderly manner. Citizens must know what to expect if they are to avoid breaking the rules. The Supreme Court has overturned prior Court rulings only about

100 times in its more than 200-year history. Changing public attitudes on which laws are acceptable in our society sometimes force the justices to admit the Court was mistaken.

The Witnesses now knew it was time to bring another flag salute case before the Court. They selected a case from West Virginia. Marie Barnette had been expelled from school for not saluting the flag, just as the Gobitas children had been. Her case was pursued through the lower courts as a class-action suit. This meant that any decisions would automatically apply to all other children in similar situations.

This time, the senior judge of the circuit court was John Parker. In ruling against the state board of education, he referred to the *Gobitis* decision. Parker wrote that normally "the decisions of the Supreme Court must be accepted by the lower courts as binding upon them if any orderly administration of justice is to be attained." But the *Gobitis* decision had been "impaired as an authority," he said, by the dissent in the *Jones* case.[16] Parker ordered West Virginian Jehovah's Witnesses allowed back into school. They would not be required to salute the flag.

The board voted to pursue the case to the Supreme Court. *West Virginia State Board of Education v. Barnette* was heard by the Court in March 1943. The members of the Court had changed in the three years since the *Gobitis* decision. Two of the justices had been replaced, including the influential Chief Justice Charles Evans Hughes. Now Harlan Stone, the sole dissenter in *Gobitis*, was chief justice.

The Court announced its decision on Flag Day, June 14, 1943. The Witnesses had finally won. The vote had been six to three. Frankfurter led the dissent, again noting that such issues should be decided by the states, not the courts.

This time, the Court based its decision chiefly on freedom of opinion and the futility of forced patriotism. "Those who begin coercive elimination of dissent soon find themselves exterminating dissenters. Compulsory unification of opinion achieves only the unanimity of the graveyard,"[17] Justice Robert Jackson wrote for the Court. He went on:

> If there is any fixed star in our constitutional
> constellation, it is that no official, high or
> petty, can prescribe what shall be orthodox in
> politics, nationalism, religion, or other matters
> of opinion or force citizens to confess by word
> or act of faith therein. . . . We think the actions
> of the local authorities in compelling the flag
> salute and pledge transcends constitutional
> limitations on their power and invades the
> sphere of intellect and spirit which it is the
> purpose of the First Amendment to our Consti-
> tution to reserve from all official control.[18]

There was little public reaction against the Witnesses this time. The horrors revealed in Nazi Germany served as a caution against the excesses of national unity and religious bigotry. People began to see the difference between forced salutes and concentration camps as only one of degree.

The *Barnette* decision has remained the primary bulwark against restrictions of freedom of religion in the United States. There have been times when calls for patriotism have threatened citizens' freedoms. The loyalty oaths required during the Communist purges of the 1950s were eventually found to be illegal. During the Vietnam War, officials again increased their emphasis on loyalty. A Connecticut teacher dismissed for refusing to say the Pledge of Allegiance during that time was reinstated because of the precedent set by *Barnette*. A local New Jersey law requiring a flag salute before speaking at town meetings was also struck down due to the ruling.

Another important Supreme Court case clarified how the free exercise clause of the First Amendment applied to schoolchildren. Jonas Yoder practiced traditional Amish ways on his farm in Wisconsin. The Amish believe in keeping to themselves and shunning modern conveniences. Their way of life is similar to that of the farming communities of the last century.

Yoder protested a Wisconsin state law requiring children to attend school until the age of sixteen. He allowed his children to go to public school until eighth grade, but then he kept them at home. He wanted his older children to help their parents with chores. Yoder needed the time to teach them basic farming skills such as carpentry, tanning, weaving, and the like.

Wisconsin authorities responded by fining Yoder and other like-minded Amish parents. The Amish believed this was a restriction of their religious freedom. Not only did it interfere with their way of life, they said, but it risked their children's heavenly salvation by teaching them sinful ways of the modern world.

When *Wisconsin v. Yoder* reached the Supreme Court in 1972, the Amish pleaded that they be allowed to preserve their way of life. Surely their values were as worthwhile as those taught by the secular authorities, the Amish argued.

The Court noted the difference in cultures:

> The high school tends to emphasize intellectual
> and scientific accomplishments, self-
> distinction, competitiveness, worldly success,

and social life with other students. Amish
society emphasizes informal learning-through-
doing, a life of "goodness," rather than a life of
intellect, wisdom, rather than technical knowl-
edge, community welfare rather than competition, and separation, rather than integration
with contemporary worldly society.[19]

The Court found those values worthy of preserving and ruled in
Yoder's favor. The justices restricted the ruling on two counts, though. It
was only because of their deeply held religious belief in that way of life that
the Amish could claim protection under the First and Fourteenth Amendments. The state's interest in requiring a few more years of formal
education was not compelling enough to override Yoder's religious freedom.

"Only those interests of the highest order," the Court said, "and those
not otherwise served can overbalance the legitimate claim to the free
exercise of religion."[20] In other words, if, and only if, the state has a
compelling interest may religious liberties be restricted. Thus human
sacrifice would not be allowed, even if it were part of a church's sacra-
ments.

The breadth of the free exercise clause in the First Amendment has
been expanded by relatively few cases, which were brought before the
Court by members of minority sects. For the moment, there is considerable
agreement among the American public as to how far that liberty extends.
This is not true of free exercise's companion clause. Just what constitutes
establishment of religion has been a matter of debate since the Bill of
Rights' passage. As we shall see, the controversy continues today.

CHAPTER FIVE

The Bible Wars

It is pitifully easy to crush out freedom in an overzealous attempt to preserve it.[1]

—Elliott Roosevelt
Radio commentator and son of
President Franklin D. Roosevelt,
deploring attacks on Jehovah's Witnesses

What some view as a violation of their First Amendment rights, others consider a part of their heritage. People have often had trouble seeing how long-entrenched customs amounted to an "establishment of religion" by the government. The controversy between the two views has been going on for decades.

During the mid-1800s, students in Cincinnati, Ohio, routinely read passages from the Bible in the public schools. When parents of different faiths challenged the practice, the Cincinnati Board of Education told the schools to stop religious readings. Other parents protested the change.

As the controversy heated up, the newspapers referred to the debate as the "Bible Wars." The issue ended up in the Ohio State Supreme Court in 1872. The court ruled the board had the right to forbid Bible reading in class. Its opinion contained a strong endorsement of church-state separation:

> [Christianity's] laws are divine, and not
> human. Its essential interests lie beyond
> the reach and range of human governments.
> United with government, religion never rises
> above the merest superstition; united with
> religion, government never rises above the
> merest despotism; and all history shows us
> that the more widely and completely they
> are separated, the better it is for both.[2]

The same issue was addressed in 1910 by the Illinois Supreme Court. Catholic parents protested readings from the Protestant Bible in public schools. The school authorities allowed students not wishing to take part in the exercise to leave the room, just as in the *Engel* case that was to follow more than 50 years later. The court banned the readings, finding "the exclusion of a pupil from this part of the school exercise in which the rest of the school joins, separates him from his fellows, puts him in a class by himself, deprives him of his equality with the other pupils, subjects him to a religious stigma, and places him at a disadvantage in the school, which was never contemplated."[3]

Some courts took the opposite stance, ruling that there were secular reasons for religious exercises. In Topeka in 1904, courts allowed a teacher to lead the class in reciting the Lord's Prayer every day. The teacher said the activity served only to quiet her class before their lessons.

This was reminiscent of an 1866 case in Massachusetts. There, a girl who refused to bow her head during school prayers was expelled. The Supreme Court of Massachusetts agreed with the school that the exercise was meant only to ensure quiet and decorum.

The Court evaded the question of public funding of churches in the 1930 case, *Cochran v. Louisiana State Board of Education.* The state supplied nonreligious textbooks to children in public and parochial schools. Taxpayers objected to this use of their money to aid religious institutions. The Court ruled that the state gave the books "to the children," not to the schools.[4]

In *Everson v. Board of Education,* decided in 1947, the Court ruled for the first time that states as well as the federal government were banned from aiding religion. A New Jersey statute allowed local school boards to reimburse parents for the cost of busing students to school. All students using public transportation were eligible, whether they attended public or parochial schools. When the Ewing Township School Board followed the policy, Arch Everson, a local taxpayer, sued. He claimed that using tax money to pay for transportation to and from parochial schools amounted to an establishment of religion.

The Supreme Court ruled against Everson, using much the same reasoning as in *Cochran.* The money, the Court noted, didn't go directly to the schools. But the Court, in an opinion written by Justice Hugo Black, set up strict limits on the government's involvement with religion:

> Neither a state nor the Federal Government
> can set up a church. Neither can pass laws
> which aid one religion, aid all religions,
> or prefer one religion over another. Neither

can force nor influence a person to go to or remain away from church against his will or force him to profess a belief or disbelief in any religion. No person can be punished for entertaining or professing religious beliefs or disbeliefs, for church attendance or non-attendance. No tax in any amount, large or small, can be levied to support any religious activities or institutions, whatever they may be called, or whatever form they may adopt to teach or practice religion.[5]

The Court received much criticism for the decision. Some claimed that, according to the opinion's logic, the Court should have ruled in Everson's favor. A minority of four of the justices thought the same way.

Many others complained that the ruling left no room for any church-state interaction. Clearly, if a church's activities interfered with other citizens' freedoms, the state must intervene, some citizens said. Even church internal affairs were liable to government action. If a congregation were to split, it might take court proceedings to divide the church's property.

The following year, the Court expanded *Everson*'s restrictions to include religious instruction in public schools. The case, *McCollum v. Board of Education*, began in 1945 in Champaign, Illinois. The local school board allowed private church groups to teach religion during regular school hours. Students were to choose Jewish, Protestant, or Roman Catholic instruction. Anyone who didn't want to attend the half-hour classes was excused.

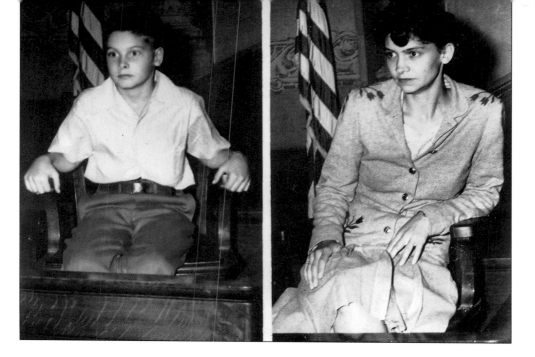

James Terry McCollum, 10, and his mother, Vashti McCollum, testify in an Urbana, Illinois, courtroom during a 1945 trial on religious instruction in public schools.

When fourth-grader James McCollum brought home a permission slip for the classes, his mother signed it. Vashti McCollum chose the Protestant group studies for James. As the year went on, she decided that the lessons conflicted with the family's religious beliefs.

The following year, McCollum kept her son out of the classes. The teachers told James to sit in the hall and read while his classmates attended religion studies. Other students teased him. They thought he was sent to sit by himself as a punishment.

McCollum didn't like others picking on her son because of a school policy. She went to court to force the school to stop teaching religion. McCollum wasn't trying to fight all religious instruction. However, as she explained, "There is such a thing as indoctrination against religion as well as indoctrination for it, and I don't believe in either."[6]

In 1947, the Illinois Supreme Court ruled against McCollum. The U.S. Supreme Court took up the case the next year. Meanwhile, the McCollum family endured vandalism, nasty phone calls and letters, and death threats. Vashti McCollum was called "a wicked, godless woman, an emissary of Satan, a Communist, and a fiend in human form."[7]

The justices were somewhat calmer in considering the issues involved. "The question to be decided is not atheism versus religious belief nor the value of religious education," wrote a *Chicago Sun-Times* columnist. "The question is whether religious instruction shall be carried on in tax-supported public schools at which attendance is compulsory; and whether the type of instruction given semi-officially takes on, in practice, the form and substance of a compulsory curriculum."[8]

The Court decided the school's action was an unconstitutional establishment of religion. Justice Black, again writing the Court's opinion, explained:

> Pupils compelled by law to go to school for secular education are released in part from their legal duty upon the condition that they attend the religious classes. This is beyond all question a utilization of the tax-established and tax-supported public school system to aid religious groups to spread their faith. And it falls squarely under the ban of the First Amendment.[9]

Black repeated the injunctions of the *Everson* opinion. At the end of the opinion, he used Jefferson's analogy as he had in the previous case:

As we said in the *Everson* case, the First Amendment has erected a wall between Church and State which must be kept high and impregnable. Here not only are the State's tax-supported public school buildings used for the dissemination of religious doctrines. The State also affords sectarian groups an invaluable aid in that it helps to provide pupils for their religious classes through use of the State's compulsory public school machinery. This is not separation of Church and State.[10]

In a concurring opinion, Justice Frankfurter pointed out the coercive nature of allowing nonparticipating students to leave the room. "The law of imitation operates," he wrote, "and non-conformity is not an outstanding characteristic of children. The result is an obvious pressure upon children to attend."[11]

Many schools throughout the country had similar "release time" programs, as they were called. In the wake of *McCollum*, school boards attempted to avoid lawsuits by using various tactics.

New York City formulated a plan almost identical to the Champaign policy. The difference was that the students attending religion classes left the school premises. Those not participating went to a study hall at the school.

This policy was also challenged. The case came before the Supreme Court in 1952 as *Zorach v. Clauson*. This time, a majority of the justices found the plan acceptable. The New York plan involved no expenditure of taxpayers' money. Children not attending religion classes weren't as likely to be stigmatized. With that in mind, the Court found no reason why the government couldn't accommodate the churches.

Justice William Douglas wrote the opinion for the Court. If the New York law were found unconstitutional, he said, students couldn't even be excused for religious holidays. Douglas wrote:

> We are a religious people whose institutions presuppose a Supreme Being. . . . When the state encourages religious instruction or cooperates with religious authorities by adjusting the schedule of public events to sectarian needs, it follows the best of our traditions. For it then respects the religious nature of our people and accommodates the public service to their spiritual needs.[12]

Three of the justices believed the New York law was still an establishment of religion. In particular, they were concerned that nonparticipating students were required to stay at school in a study hall. Robert Jackson, one of the dissenting justices, complained that the school "serves as a temporary jail for a student who will not go to church."[13] He added, "The day that this country ceases to be free for irreligion it will cease to be free for religion—except for that sect that can win political power."[14]

As the decade wore on, more and more school-religion cases arose in the states. Clearly, it was only a matter of time before the Court had to address the issue. By 1958, the scene was set for *Engel v. Vitale*—one of the key Supreme Court religion cases—to begin its journey to the Supreme Court.

CHAPTER SIX

The Roths Fight Back

A union of government and religion tends to destroy government and to degrade religion.[1]

—Justice Hugo Black

When Lawrence Roth organized his group of parents, morning exercises like the Regents' prayer were common throughout the country. Often, students recited the Lord's Prayer after the Pledge of Allegiance before classes began.

There was an important difference in the New York case, though. The parents' lawyer explained, "This was the first time in the history of the United States that a state had actually composed a prayer and then inserted this prayer into one of its compulsory institutions."[2]

William Vitale certainly never believed the prayer would be so controversial. "The teachers were to be instructed that this was not necessarily a compelling thing," the Herricks school board president said. "If a child for some basic reason chose to be excused, he or she would be excused."[3]

When Vitale told the other school board members about the parents' petition, they decided to fight it. Bertram Daiker, the board's attorney, began compiling his defense. His opponent was William Butler, a conservative corporate lawyer on the board of the New York Civil Liberties Union, the local chapter of the ACLU.

Butler later recalled how he was selected: "When the case came up, they decided that the lawyer could not be a Jew. He must be Catholic, that is, someone taking the attitude that he is DEFENDING prayer and religious freedom, not attacking it. And they looked down at the end of the table and saw a nice Irish-Catholic boy—William Butler."[4] Butler was assisted by Stanley Geller, another ACLU lawyer.

The ACLU wanted a group representing diverse religious beliefs. That way, any judgment reached would have broad impact. The parents' group included two Jews and a Unitarian. Another was a member of the Ethical Culture Union, a movement that believes in the supremacy of moral law and promotes social reforms. The fifth member was an atheist, a person who denies the existence of God.

The Supreme Court had ruled in 1961 that even "religions in this country which do not teach what would generally be considered a belief in the existence of God [such as] Buddhism, Taoism, Ethical Culture, Secular Humanism and others,"[5] had to be treated as religions in applying the Constitution's religious protections. The same ruling, *Torcaso v. Watkins*, applied to atheists.

Roth was classified as an atheist for the suit, though that label was questionable. "I would classify myself as a very religious person, but not a churchgoer," Roth said. "I have prayed myself, many times—not in a beseeching manner, but more in seeking guidance."[6] Roth added, "I was born a Jew, but I believe in a Creative Process. And I'm not at all sure we can change anything by petitioning to a higher being. So when affiliation came up, I explained the way I felt to Butler and he said, 'You're the atheist!' Apparently you have to have an atheist in the crowd so we started from there."[7]

Roth's group wasn't the only party interested in prayer in the Herricks schools. Henry Hollenberg, an Orthodox Jew, rallied other parents to support the prayer policy. They hired Porter Chandler, an attorney with experience representing the Catholic Church.

Butler, Daiker, and Chandler submitted their briefs to the New York Supreme Court. (In New York, the supreme court is the lowest-level court with jurisdiction over such cases.) The hearing was held in Nassau County Court House in early 1959. Judge Bernard Meyer listened to the lawyers' arguments and began his deliberations. It was six months before Roth and the others learned his decision.

Judge Meyer's opinion was equivocal. Although he ruled in the school board's favor, he included this warning: "The 'establishment' clause of the Constitution does not prohibit the non-compulsory saying of the Regents' Prayer in the public schools, but . . . the 'free exercise' clause requires that [the school] board take affirmative steps to protect the rights of those who, for whatever reason, choose not to participate."[8] Meyer suggested perhaps allowing nonparticipating students to arrive at school after the prayer was over.

Roth was disappointed. "It seemed strange to me that a judge would render a decision saying . . . 'this prayer is legal but if you do so and so it's going to be even more legal,'"[9] he said.

Butler was more philosophical. He realized that an early loss could pave the way for a bigger win later. If the school board had lost, the board members might have decided the school district could not afford an appeal to the next higher court. The ACLU had larger resources and was willing

63

William Butler, *left,* the ACLU lawyer who argued the *Engel* case for the five parents who opposed the Regents' prayer, and Bertram Daiker, attorney for the Herricks school board

to appeal the case all the way to the U.S. Supreme Court. As the losing party, the parents' group could force the school board back into court.

Butler admitted later that he was "scared that we might win in the lower courts. That way we would not have had a national decision. One way to cut the bridges of a civil libertarian quickly is to render a decision in the lower court."[10]

Butler next took his argument to the Appellate Division of the New York Supreme Court. There he did no better. The school board won again. Time wore on. It began to look like some of the children involved in the case would be out of school before a final decision had been reached.

Daniel Roth later recalled that teachers resented the brothers more than the students did. "I definitely remember an antagonism from the teachers, no question about that. There were comments made. I remember an eighth-grade teacher in particular. She would make snide remarks about what my father was doing. . . . I was certainly singled out by her for humiliation."[11]

Butler had to exhaust all appeals at the state level before moving on to the U.S. Supreme Court. There was one step left to go. The New York State Court of Appeals ruled on the case in 1961. Again the court decided against Roth's group. Chief Judge Charles S. Desmond wrote the opinion. "Saying this simple prayer may be, according to the broadest possible dictionary definition, an act of 'religion,' but when the Founding Fathers prohibited 'an establishment of religion' they were referring to official adoption of, or favor to, one or more sects,"[12] he wrote.

But this time, it was a divided court. Two of the seven judges on the court dissented. The dissent contended that the Regents' prayer "cannot help but lead to a gradual erosion of the mighty bulwark erected by the First Amendment,"[13] and therefore was unconstitutional.

Butler was encouraged. A written dissent from an appeals court gave his arguments more legitimacy. Now he needed to convince a majority of the men sitting on the nation's highest court.

After the defeat in the court of appeals, Butler and Geller filed a petition asking the U.S. Supreme Court to review the case. Daiker submitted a brief for the school board and Hollenberg's group opposing the appeal.

The Board of Regents also filed an amicus brief defending the prayer policy. The board's counsel, Charles Brind, wrote that the Regents were "aware of the dire need, in these days of concentrated attacks by an atheistic way of life upon our world . . . of finding ways to pass on America's Moral and Spiritual Heritage to our youth through the public school system."[14]

On December 4, 1961, the Court voted to hear the case. When at least four of the justices vote that a case merits a hearing, the Court grants a writ of certiorari. This is an order that the certified records of the last court to hear the case be forwarded to the Supreme Court. The Court scheduled oral arguments in the case for April 3, 1962.

In the meantime, a federal court decision in Pennsylvania offered Butler some hope. In 1959, Edward Schempp had sued to prevent the Abington Township School Board from requiring Bible reading in school. Schempp was a Unitarian with two children in high school. The Bible reading was against his religious convictions.

The court decided in Schempp's favor. The decision outlawed the Pennsylvania Public School Act of 1949. This statute required the reading of ten or more Bible verses at the start of every school day.

At Abington High School, the readings were broadcast over the intercom. The school provided a King James Bible. Students reading the verses could bring a Catholic or Jewish version of the Bible if they wanted to. There was no commentary or interpretation of the Bible verses. The reader then recited the Lord's Prayer and the Pledge of Allegiance. The other students were expected to join in.

After the 1959 court decision, the Pennsylvania legislature amended the law. Students could now leave the room if they decided not to participate. Schempp sued again. He didn't want his children to have to leave the room. He thought that would damage their relationship with fellow students and teachers.

On February 1, 1962, the same federal court found the amended version of the act still unconstitutional. Chief Judge John Biggs Jr. wrote, "The fact that some pupils, or theoretically all pupils, might be excused from attendance at the exercise does not mitigate the obligatory nature of the ceremony. . . . Since the statute required the reading of the 'Holy Bible,' a Christian document, the practice . . . prefers the Christian religion."[15]

Such a finding by a federal court could only help Butler's case. On the morning of the oral arguments, he was fairly confident but not certain he would win. Supreme Court hearings begin on a traditional note. As the justices file out from behind the long velvet curtains to take their places at the bench, the Court crier announces them. This time there was an irony in his words. "Oyez, Oyez, Oyez. God save the United States and this honorable court."[16]

The Board of Regents' brief had cited the customary opening words of the Court proceedings as proof that religion was acceptable in government affairs. When Butler stood to address the Court, Justice Douglas asked, "This courtroom, where we have an announcement every time we come— 'God save the United States and this honorable Court,' we haven't decided whether that's constitutional or not, have we?"[17] Butler admitted this was so.

"We have not decided whether compulsory prayer in the halls of Congress is constitutional," Douglas continued. "Is that case on its way here?"

Butler replied, "If it is, Your Honor, I'm glad I'm not bringing it."[18] Both men were aware of the passions aroused by the hearing's topic. Butler launched into his argument:

> I want to make it absolutely clear before this
> Court that I come here not as an antagonist of
> religion, that my clients are deeply religious
> people; that we come here in the firm belief
> that the best safety of religion in the United

The room where the Supreme Court justices hear cases

States, and freedom of religion, is to keep
religion out of our public life and not to con-
found, as Roger Williams said, the civil with
the religious. . . . My clients say that prayer is
good. But what we say here is, it's the begin-

ning of the end of religious freedom when religious activity such as this is incorporated into the public school system of the United States.[19]

Butler then pointed out the coercive nature of school prayer:

> Would the little child, would "Johnny," leave the classroom; or would the parent be expected to ask the school system to excuse his child, who may be singled out as a non-conformist? I must adopt Mr. Justice Frankfurter's thesis in *McCollum* that the law of imitation applies. Little children want to be with other little children. . . . The effect would be to cast upon this child's mind some indelible mark, and I think it can be sustained that, in effect, the children are coerced into saying this prayer, because of these reasons.[20]

Butler next argued against the contentions set out in his opponents' briefs. He said the Court's finding in *Zorach* didn't apply to *Engel*. The former case involved schools' accommodation of churches. The Regents' prayer, he said, was direct government participation in religion.

The school board had stressed that parents who objected to the prayer were a tiny minority. The implication was that, in a democracy, the majority should rule. Butler countered that "the very purpose of the Constitution is to protect the minority against the majority, to protect the weak against the strong in matters of keeping separate forever the functions of the civil and the religious."[21]

Bertram Daiker's turn came next. He emphasized the noncompulsory nature of the school's morning exercises. "Those children who do not wish to join in the prayer or whose parents do not wish them to join in the prayer may remain seated; they may remain silent,"[22] he said.

Daiker continued:

> Since the earliest days of this country, going
> back to the Mayflower Compact, the men who
> put the country together have publicly and
> repeatedly recognized the existence of a Su-
> preme Being, a God. When, therefore, we say
> here this prayer . . . we are proceeding fully in
> accord with the tradition and heritage that has
> been handed down to us. . . . We are not trying
> here in the Herricks School District to teach
> religion . . . any more than . . . the prayer used
> in this Court.[23]

Next up was Porter Chandler, representing Hollenberg's group of parents supporting the prayer. He passionately pleaded their case:

> Why are my clients here at all? They are here
> in the name of the free exercise of religion, if
> you want to put it that way. They are here
> because they feel very strongly that it is a
> deprivation of their children's right to share in

our national heritage, and that it is a compulsory rewriting of our history in the fashion of George Orwell's *1984* to do what these petitioners are now seeking to do, namely to eliminate all reference to God from the whole fabric of our public life and of our public educational system.[24]

The justices had few questions for Daiker or Chandler. The arguments over, the justices retired to deliberate. The lawyers, the parents, and the whole nation waited tensely for their decision. Meanwhile, another important case came closer to a rendezvous with the Court.

On that same day, April 3, Maryland's Court of Appeals ruled that a Baltimore school Bible reading policy was constitutional. Morning exercises were similar to those in the Abington case. Madalyn Murray had requested that her son, William, be excused from the activity. Both were atheists. When she saw how he was ostracized for not taking part in the activity, she sued to stop the Bible reading.

Murray claimed that the policy violated the First Amendment. She also said that her son, as an atheist, was denied the equal protection of law guaranteed by the Fourteenth Amendment. In a four-to-three decision, the court denied Murray's request.

Judge William Horney, writing for the court, explained the decision:

Neither the First nor the Fourteenth Amendment was intended to stifle all rapport between religion and Government. The Supreme Court of the United States has not yet passed on

either of the constitutional questions posed by
this appeal. Yet there are several decisions
concerning the separation of church and state
which we think point the way and clearly
indicate that a public school opening exercise
such as this one—where the time and money
spent on it is inconsequential—does not violate
the [two amendments] as would the teaching of
a sectarian religion in a public school on school
time and at public expense.[25]

Chief Judge Frederick Brune wrote the dissent for the minority. He called the Bible reading "directly contrary to the prohibition against any 'law respecting an establishment of religion,' contained in the First Amendment, as that provision has been interpreted by the Supreme Court."[26]

Less than three months later, on June 25, 1962, the Supreme Court ruled in the *Engel* case. The Court, in a six to one decision, declared the use of the Regents' prayer in class unconstitutional. Roth and the other parents had won.

Only Justice Potter Stewart dissented. He argued, in his dissent, that denying children the right to recite the Regents' prayer "is to deny them the opportunity of sharing in the spiritual heritage of our Nation." Simply allowing children to say the prayer, Stewart said, did not mean the school board had established an "official religion."

Justices Felix Frankfurter and Byron White took no part in deciding the case.

Justice Black wrote in the majority opinion, "We think that by using its public school system to encourage recitation of the Regents' prayer, the

State of New York has adopted a practice wholly inconsistent with the Establishment Clause. There can, of course, be no doubt that New York's program of daily classroom invocation of God's blessings as prescribed in the Regents' prayer is a religious activity."[27]

Black further noted:

> We think that the constitutional prohibition against laws respecting an establishment of religion must at least mean that in this country it is no part of the business of government to compose official prayers for any group of the American people to recite as part of a religious program carried on by government. It is a matter of history that this very practice of establishing governmentally composed prayers for religious services was one of the reasons which caused many of our early colonists to leave England and seek religious freedom in America. . . . There were men of this same faith in the power of prayer who led the fight for adoption of our Constitution and also for our Bill of Rights with the very guarantees of religious freedom that forbid the sort of governmental activity which New York has attempted here.[28]

Black spoke of the founders' motivation in keeping religion separate from government: "an awareness that governments of the past had shackled men's tongues to make them speak only the religious thoughts that government wanted them to speak and to pray only to the God that government wanted them to pray to."[29]

Black went on to discuss the First Amendment's role in preserving citizens' religious freedom. "The First Amendment was added to the Constitution to stand as a guarantee that neither the power nor the prestige of the Federal Government would be used to control, support or influence the kinds of prayer the American people can say,"[30] he said.

The opinion dismissed the Regents' efforts to ensure the legality of the school prayer by making it optional and nonsectarian. Even if this were true, Black said, a state-mandated prayer was still unconstitutional. He wrote, "Neither the fact that the prayer may be denominationally neutral nor the fact that its observance on the part of the students is voluntary can serve to free it from the limitations of the Establishment Clause."[31]

Black went on to condemn the inherent coercion of school prayer. "When the power, prestige and financial support of government is placed behind a particular religious belief, the indirect coercive pressure upon religious minorities to conform to the prevailing officially approved religion is plain,"[32] he wrote.

Black understood the furor the Court's decision would create. He tried to quiet fears that the *Engel* decision was a victory for atheism:

> It has been argued that to apply the Constitution in such a way as to prohibit state laws respecting an establishment of religious services in public schools is to indicate a hostility toward religion or toward prayer. Nothing, of course, could be more wrong. . . . It is neither

sacrilegious nor antireligious to say that each separate government in this country should stay out of the business of writing or sanctioning official prayers and leave that purely religious function to the people themselves and to those the people choose to look to for religious guidance.[33]

Finally, Black addressed those who did not see how a voluntary, blandly worded prayer could threaten Americans' freedoms. The opinion concluded, "To those who may subscribe to the view that because the Regents' official prayer is so brief and general there can be no danger to religious freedom in its governmental establishment, however, it may be appropriate to say in the words of James Madison, the author of the First Amendment: 'It is proper to take alarm at the first experiment on our liberties.'"[34]

He went on to repeat Madison's warning that if one group could establish Christianity as the state religion, another group could easily set up a particular sect of Christianity and exclude all others.

Students from around the country stand with their heads bowed before the United States Supreme Court in Washington, D.C., in a demonstration supporting prayer in public schools.

CHAPTER SEVEN

The **Battle** *for* **School** **Prayer**

Whilst we assert for ourselves a free-
dom to embrace, to profess and to
observe the Religion which we believe
to be of divine origin, we cannot deny
an equal freedom to those whose minds
have not yet yielded to the evidence
that has convinced us. If this freedom
be abused, it is an offence against
God, not against man.[1]

—James Madison

Reaction to the decision was immediate. Newspaper
headlines throughout the country proclaimed: SCHOOL PRAYER UNCONSTITU-
TIONAL, BAN PRAYER IN PUBLIC SCHOOLS, and SCHOOL PRAYER HELD ILLEGAL.[2]
Editorials decried the decision as a sign of moral decay. Many church
leaders condemned the Supreme Court as godless.

In the following days, 177 bills were introduced in both houses of Congress to reinstate the prayer by constitutional amendment. One congressman suggested that school boards across the country set aside one minute for students to pray silently that the Court would reverse the ruling.

President John F. Kennedy tried to quiet the acrimony, while supporting the decision. "It is important for us, if we're going to maintain our constitutional principle, that we support Supreme Court decisions even when we may not agree with them. In addition, we have in this case a very easy remedy, and that is to pray ourselves,"[3] he said. "And I would think that it would be a welcome reminder to every American family that we can pray a good deal more at home, and we can attend our churches with a good deal more fidelity, and we can make the true meaning of prayer much more important in the lives of all our children."[4]

Many believed that the opinion would lead to a disappearance of all religion from public life. To them, the decision seemed at odds with the nation's patriotic songs, its official oaths, even the motto on its coins—"In God We Trust."

The Court had foreseen this criticism. In a footnote to the *Engel* opinion, Black tried to limit any broad application of the ruling:

> There is of course nothing in the decision reached here that is inconsistent with the fact that school children and others are officially encouraged to express love for our country by reciting historical documents such as the Declaration of Independence which contain references to the Deity or by singing officially espoused anthems which include the composer's

Joseph Roth, taken in 1986

professions of faith in a Supreme Being, or with
the fact that there are many manifestations in
our public life of belief in God. Such patriotic
or ceremonial occasions bear no true resem-
blance to the unquestioned religious exercise
that the State of New York has sponsored in
this instance.[5]

Protests against the Roth family increased. "We got calls, 'Don't start
your car; it'll blow up,'" recalls Lawrence Roth. "Once, kids with gas-
soaked rags laid out a cross on our lawn, lit it, and left. Our neighbor put
it out. There were a lot of threats and picketing. Right after the decision
came out, people marched with signs, ROTH—GODLESS ATHEIST."[6]

Joseph Roth, who in 1995 was a top executive in the motion picture
industry, remembers the harassment he and his family had endured. He

was branded the devil by local ministers. Someone planted a bomb in the family's basement. Even the FBI followed him. "What saved me was that I played three sports, and the kids couldn't come to terms with a lefty-commie bad kid who was playing ball with everybody."[7]

Over the next year, the uproar slowly died down. Meanwhile, the two cases from Pennsylvania and Maryland came before the Supreme Court. The Court considered *Abington School District v. Schempp* and *Murray v. Curlett* together. It announced the single decision for the two cases on June 17, 1963.

Both Bible reading and the recitation of the Lord's Prayer in school were held to be unconstitutional. The furor erupted again. The *Engel* opinion had relied on the fact that the Regents' prayer was composed by the state. Now the *Abington* decision seemed to ban any religious text or prayer from schools.

The states attempted to justify the religious exercises by saying they had a secular purpose. These included "the promotion of moral values, the contradiction to the materialistic trends of our times, the perpetuation of our institutions and the teaching of literature."[8]

The Court found nothing wrong with these purposes. They disagreed that the readings and prayers had no religious purpose, however. Justice Tom C. Clark wrote for the Court:

> Nothing we have said here indicates that such
> study of the Bible or of religion, when pre-
> sented objectively as part of a secular program
> of education, may not be effected consistently
> with the First Amendment. But the exercises
> here do not fall into those categories. They are

religious exercises, required by the States in violation of the command of the First Amendment that the Government maintain strict neutrality, neither aiding nor opposing religion.[9]

As the concept of church-state separation has evolved in the succeeding years, it is primarily the idea of strict neutrality that has guided the courts. Many school districts across the country ignored the 1962 and 1963 Court rulings. Particularly in rural areas, the citizens tended to be devout and belonged to similar faiths. Community leaders believed they best served the needs of the townsfolk by continuing religious readings in schools. They believed that in a democracy, majority rule justified a practice most people wanted.

The *Abington* decision addressed that belief:

We cannot accept that the concept of neutrality, which does not permit a State to require a religious exercise even with the consent of the majority of those affected, collides with the majority's right to free exercise of religion. While the Free Exercise Clause clearly prohibits the use of state action to deny the rights of free exercise to anyone, it has never meant that a majority could use the machinery of the State to practice its beliefs.[10]

In other words, if even one parent found a prayer or devotional reading objectionable, the courts were bound to ban it. Even something as innocent as the "Cookie Prayer" was unacceptable. This case arose when an Illinois kindergarten teacher led her class in saying grace every day before their morning snack. The words, widely known, are:

We thank you for the flowers so sweet;
We thank you for the food we eat;
We thank you for the birds that sing;
We thank you, God, for everything.[11]

The teacher, seeking to avoid trouble, left out the word *God* in the prayer. In *DeKalb School District v. DeSpain*, a federal court found even this mild thanksgiving to be banned under the establishment clause.

A previous U.S. District Court case from New York had involved the same prayer. This time the word *God* was left in. However, in that case, authorities claimed the prayer was "student-initiated." The court still prohibited the prayer reading. The opinion noted that "in the context of closely organized schooling of young children, 'student-initiated' prayers are an illusion."[12]

The Cookie Prayer decision made people aware of the limits placed on religious activity in the schools. Many school boards scrambled to divest themselves of any appearance of helping churches. One New York school board sued the state commissioner of education, James Allen. The board sought relief from a statute requiring them to provide textbooks to all students in their district. This included parochial students. The board thought this was a conflict of church and state.

The case came before the Supreme Court in 1968 as *Board of Education v. Allen*. The Court decided that the practice was allowable. Not all teaching in church schools is religious, the justices noted. The textbooks taught strictly nonreligious subjects. The state did not single out parochial schools for special treatment. The books were available to all students in the state.

Encouraged by the *Allen* decision, some states tried to expand their aid to church schools. Pennsylvania and Rhode Island began contributing to parochial schoolteachers' salaries. Angry taxpayers brought these cases to the Supreme Court in 1971 as *Lemon v. Kurtzman*. The Court ruled against the states. In the decision, the Court formulated a three-part test to determine the constitutionality of laws involving religion. The opinion reads, "First, the statute must have a secular legislative purpose; second, its principal or primary effect must be one that neither advances nor inhibits religion . . . finally, the statute must not foster 'an excessive government entanglement with religion.'"[13]

The "*Lemon* test" has since become the primary yardstick for measuring the legality of such statutes. In *Stone v. Graham*, the U.S. Supreme Court ruled in 1980 that Kentucky could not require the Ten Commandments to be posted in classrooms. The state law that required the posting also called for a notation at the bottom of the display that read: "The secular application of the Ten Commandments is clearly seen in its adoption as the fundamental legal code of Western Civilization and the Common Law of the United States."[14]

The Court found the display "plainly religious in nature. The Ten Commandments are undeniably a sacred text in Jewish and Christian faiths, and no legislative recitation of a supposed secular purpose can blind us to that fact,"[15] scolded the justices.

In the same year, a U.S. Court of Appeals upheld that Christmas pageants and similar festivities are allowable at schools. The judges in

Florey v. Sioux Falls District realized how fine a line they were treading, though. "We recognize that this opinion . . . will not resolve for all times, places or circumstances the question of when Christmas carols, or other music or drama having religious themes, can be sung or performed by students in elementary and secondary schools without offending the First Amendment,"[16] the opinion read.

A U.S. District Court cited the *Lemon* test in considering a complaint brought by several students in 1976. At stake was a Massachusetts law that read:

> At the commencement of the first class of each
> day in all grades in all public schools the
> teacher in charge of the room in which each
> such class is held shall announce that a period
> of silence not to exceed one minute in duration
> shall be observed for meditation or prayer, and
> during any such period silence shall be main-
> tained and no activities engaged in.[17]

The students thought the moment of silence violated the principles set forth in *Engel* and *Abington*. Judge Frank Murray, writing for the court, found it did not. "In our view plaintiffs have failed to show the absence of a neutral, secular purpose for the opening moment of silence," he wrote. "The statute and guidelines do not have a primary effect of favoring or sponsoring religion. They do not involve the state in religious exercises or directly in the realm of religion. They do not fall within the proscriptions of the First Amendment."[18]

State and federal courts struck down similar statutes. In 1982,

Tennessee tried to pass a statute similar to the Massachusetts law mandating a moment of silence for meditation or prayer. The U.S. District Court decided the measure was illegal. The court objected to the intended purpose of the moment of silence—"meditation or prayer."

Even if the language was ambiguous, the judges said, the purpose was not. The court examined the legislative proceedings leading up to the measure. The record clearly showed the state was merely trying to provide a means for teachers to lead students in prayer.

A U.S. District Court decision in New Mexico the following year came to the same conclusion. "Moment of silence" statutes would be subject to scrutiny of the legislature's purpose. The court considered the New Mexico law's wording "a transparent ruse meant to divert attention from the statute's true purpose."[19]

A similar New Jersey statute tried to avoid the problem by not using the word *prayer*. The students were to use the moment of silence "for quiet and private contemplation or introspection."[20] An examination of the record convinced a U.S. District Court to overturn the statute:

> All the evidence points to the religious intent of
> this enactment—the period of more than a
> decade during which the New Jersey legislature
> sought to evade *Engel* and *Abington Township*
> in order to reintroduce a mandatory time for
> prayer in the public schools; the debate upon
> the Bill which was in terms of public prayer
> and State involvement in religion; the time and
> manner in which the minute of silence was
> mandated, following the form and posture of

school prayer which was outlawed in the early 1960's.[21]

The U.S. Supreme Court finally made such "moment of silence" statutes illegal nationwide in 1985. In *Wallace v. Jaffree*, the Court referred to the legislative purpose of its own *Lemon* test. The Court found the Alabama legislature was simply trying to sneak school prayer in the back door.

The Court has come under much criticism for second-guessing the intent of a legislative body. Many legal scholars believe that a law should be judged on the merits of its language alone. For now, though, the *Wallace* decision stands.

Controversy about church-state issues continues today. Despite setbacks, many municipalities still are trying to introduce prayer into their schools. Many more areas quietly continue the practice unchallenged. Members of Congress continue to propose constitutional amendments legalizing school prayer.

The debate will go on. The ghosts of Madison, Jefferson, and their fellows may look down at us struggling with the legacy of the great First Amendment. If so, they would surely heed the words of William Butler. Worried that a school prayer amendment might ultimately threaten Americans' liberties, Butler frets, "I don't think it's possible to tinker around with the First Amendment nowadays. If the First Amendment came up today, it wouldn't pass. Thank God we are stuck with it."[22]

Source **N**otes

Chapter One

    1. Fred W. Friendly and Martha J. H. Elliott, *The Constitution: That Delicate Balance* (New York: Random House, 1984), p. 112.

    2. Ibid., p. 119.

    3. Ibid., p. 110.

    4. *New York Times* (December 5, 1961), p. 33.

    5. Arthur S. Link, Robert V. Remini, Douglas Greenberg, and Robert C. McMath Jr., *A Concise History of the American People* (Arlington Heights, Ill.: Harlan Davidson, 1984), p. A-8.

    6. Gary E. McCuen, *Religion and Politics: Issues in Religious Liberty* (Hudson, Wis.: Gary E. McCuen Publications, 1989), p. 86.

    7. Friendly and Elliott, p. 118.

Chapter Two

    1. Link et al., p. A-1.

    2. Ann E. Weiss, *God and Government: The Separation of Church and State* (Boston: Houghton Mifflin, 1982), p. 16.

    3. Friendly and Elliott, p. 111.

    4. Weiss, p. 12.

    5. Ibid., p. 18.

    6. McCuen, p. 69.

    7. Weiss, p. 23.

    8. Link et al., p. A-6.

    9. Ibid., p. A-8.

    10. McCuen, p. 91.

11. John M. Swomley Jr., *Religion, the State and the Schools* (New York: Pegasus, 1968), p. 19.

12. McCuen, p. 91.

13. Swomley, p. 19.

14. Ibid.

15. Lena E. Patterson, *Separation of Church and State* (Dayton, Oh.: Pamphlet Publications, 1984), p. 19.

16. Weiss, p. 29.

17. Link et al., p. A-8.

Chapter Three

1. Weiss, p. 33.

2. McCuen, p. 89.

3. Ibid., p. 69.

4. Victoria Sherrow, *Separation of Church and State* (New York: Franklin Watts, 1992), p. 32.

5. Ibid., p. 21.

6. Ibid., p. 38.

7. Ibid., p. 40.

8. Ibid., p. 38.

9. Link et al., p. A-9.

Chapter Four

1. *The Holy Bible* (Revised Standard Version), (New York: Williams Collins Sons, 1952), II, p. 23.

2. Harold W. Chase and Craig R. Ducat, *Constitutional Interpretation: Cases—Essays—Materials* (St. Paul, Minn.: West Publishing, 1974), p. 1306.

3. Sherrow, p. 82.

4. Leonard A. Stevens, *Salute!: The Case of The Bible vs. The Flag* (New York: Coward, McCann and Geoghegan, 1973), p. 38.

5. Ibid., p. 43.

6. Ibid., p. 50.

7. Ibid., p. 53.

8. Ibid., p. 60.

9. Ibid., p. 64.

10. Ibid., p. 71.

11. Ibid., p. 99.

12. Ibid., p. 101.

13. Ibid., p. 104.

14. Ibid., p. 124.

15. Dorothy Marquardt, *A Guide to the Supreme Court* (New York, Bobbs-Merrill, 1977), p. 15.

16. Stevens, p. 130.

17. Friendly and Elliott, p. 115.

18. Stevens, p. 134.

19. Chase and Ducat, p. 1350.

20. Leo Pfeffer, *God, Caesar, and the Constitution: The Court As Referee of Church-State Confrontation* (Boston: Beacon Press, 1975), p. 35.

Chapter Five

1. Stevens, p. 112.

2. Sherrow, p. 42.

3. Ibid., p. 43.

4. Swomley, p. 208.

5. Chase and Ducat, p. 1301.

6. Sherrow, p. 47.

7. Ibid.

8. Ibid.

9. Haig A. Bosmajian, ed., *Freedom of Religion* (New York: Neal-Schuman, 1987), p. 8.

10. Ibid., p. 9.

11. Friendly and Elliott, p. 117.

12. Leonard W. Levy, *The Establishment Clause: Religion and the First Amendment* (New York: Macmillan, 1986), p. 146.

13. Sherrow, p. 48.

14. Levy, p. 147.

Chapter Six

1. Bosmajian, p. 13.

2. Friendly and Elliott, p. 119.

3. Ibid., p. 118.

4. Ibid.

5. McCuen, p. 104.

6. *New York Times* (June 28, 1962), p. 17.

7. Friendly and Elliott, p. 119.

8. Ibid., p. 120.

9. Ibid.

10. Ibid., p. 121.

11. Ibid., p. 119.

12. Ibid., p. 121.

13. Ibid.

14. *New York Times* (Dec. 5, 1961), p. 33.

15. *New York Times* (Feb. 2, 1962), p. 31.

16. Friendly and Elliott, p. 121.

17. Ibid.

18. Ibid., p. 122.

19. Ibid.

20. Ibid.

21. Ibid.

22. Ibid., p. 123.

23. Ibid.

24. Ibid., p. 124.

25. *New York Times* (April 7, 1962), p. 14.

26. Ibid.

27. Bosmajian, p. 12.

28. Ibid.

29. Ibid., p. 14.

30. Ibid., p. 13.

31. Ibid.

32. Ibid.

33. Ibid.

34. Ibid., p. 14.

Chapter Seven

1. Stephen L. Carter, *The Culture of Disbelief* (New York: Basic Books, 1993), p. 116.

2. Sherrow, p. 49.

3. *New York Times* (July 1, 1962), IV, p. 9.

4. Sherrow, p. 50.

5. Bosmajian, p. 16.

6. Friendly and Elliott, p. 126.

7. *Newsweek*, vol. 119 (May 25, 1992), p. 63.

8. Bosmajian, p. 23.

9. Ibid.

10. Ibid.

11. Pfeffer, p. 203.

12. Bosmajian, p. 27.

13. Chase and Ducat, p. 1325.

14. Bosmajian, p. 92.

15. Ibid.

16. Ibid., p. 78.

17. Ibid., p. 38.

18. Ibid.

19. Ibid., p. 111.

20. Ibid., p. 115.

21. Ibid., p. 122.

22. Friendly and Elliott, p. 126.

Further Reading

Beggs, David W. III, and R. Bruch McQuigg. *America's Schools and Churches: Partners in Conflict.* Bloomington, Ind.: University of Indiana Press, 1965.

Bosmajian, Haig A., ed. *Freedom of Religion.* New York: Neal-Schuman, 1987.

Bowen, Catherine Drinker. *Miracle in Philadelphia: The Story of the Constitutional Convention, May to September 1787.* Boston: Atlantic Monthly Press, 1986.

Carter, Stephen L. *The Culture of Disbelief.* New York: Basic Books, 1993.

Coy, Harold (revised by Lorna Greenberg). *The Supreme Court.* New York: Franklin Watts, 1981.

Faber, Doris, and Harold Faber. *We the People: The Story of the Constitution Since 1787.* New York: Scribners, 1987.

Forte, David F. *The Supreme Court.* New York: Franklin Watts, 1979.

Fribourg, Marjorie G. *The Supreme Court in American History: Ten Great Decisions—The People, the Times and the Issues.* Philadelphia: Macrae Smith, 1965.

Friendly, Fred W., and Martha J. H. Elliott. The *Constitution: That Delicate Balance.* New York: Random House, 1984.

Gaustad, Edwin Scott. *A Religious History of America.* New York: Harper and Row, 1975.

Goode, Stephen. *The Controversial Court: Supreme Court Influences on American Life.* New York: Julian Messner, 1982.

Greene, Carol. *The Supreme Court.* Chicago: Childrens Press, 1985.

Harrison, Maureen, and Steve Gilbert, eds. *Landmark Decisions of the United States Supreme Court*. Beverly Hills, Cal.: Excellent Books, 1991.

Hill, Samuel S., and Dennis E. Owen. *The New Religious Political Right in America*. Nashville, Tenn.: Abingdon, 1982.

Kleeberg, Irene Cumming. *Separation of Church and State*. New York: Franklin Watts, 1986.

Lawson, Don. *Landmark Supreme Court Cases*. Hillside, N.J.: Enslow, 1987.

Marnell, William H. *The First Amendment: The History of Religious Freedom in America*. New York: Doubleday, 1964.

Marquardt, Dorothy A. *A Guide to the Supreme Court*. Indianapolis: Bobbs-Merrill, 1977.

McCuen, Gary E. *Religion and Politics: Issues in Religious Liberty*. Hudson, Wis.: Gary E. McCuen, 1989.

Patterson, Lena E. *Separation of Church and State*. Dayton, Oh.: Pamphlet Publications, 1984.

Sherrow, Victoria. *Separation of Church and State*. New York: Franklin Watts, 1992.

Stein, R. Conrad. *The Story of the Powers of the Supreme Court*. Chicago: Childrens Press, 1989.

Stevens, Leonard A. *Salute!: The Case of the Bible vs. the Flag*. New York: Coward, McCann and Geoghegan, 1973.

Swomley, John M. Jr. *Religion, the State and the Schools*. New York: Pegasus, 1968.

Weiss, Ann E. *God and Government: The Separation of Church and State*. Boston: Houghton Mifflin, 1982.

Index